EMILY'S STORY

WHAT SHOULD I SAY OR HOW SHOULD I SAY IT?

EMILY J. COOPWOOD

authorHOUSE

AuthorHouse™
1663 Liberty Drive
Bloomington, IN 47403
www.authorhouse.com
Phone: 833-262-8899

Published by AuthorHouse 05/21/2021

ISBN: 978-1-6655-2677-7 (sc)
ISBN: 978-1-6655-2675-3 (hc)
ISBN: 978-1-6655-2676-0 (e)

Library of Congress Control Number: 2021910312

Print information available on the last page.

*Any people depicted in stock imagery provided
by Getty Images are models, and such images are
being used for illustrative purposes only.
Certain stock imagery* © *Getty Images.*

This book is printed on acid-free paper.

*Scripture quotations marked KJV are from the Holy Bible,
King James Version (Authorized Version). First published
in 1611. Quoted from the KJV Classic Reference Bible,
Copyright* © *1983 by The Zondervan Corporation.*

INTRODUCTION

God's Grace and Mercy is always in the midst of the battle of the war going on in our minds that affects us both naturally and spiritually. Everyone has conflict and at times we do not see the light. However, God knows our struggles and promised that He would never leave us alone.

This is a story of my journey through the maze of my life that unfolded in many directions. A story where the results were so amazing to see as God orchestrated every step as I dared to visualize and believe!

THE BEGINNING

My parents married in 1925 and built a home in a neighborhood, which at that time, had developed with several different nationalities. I was born in that home along with my only brother, Walter. We were blessed to have good parents, a grandmother who lived with us, and were never left alone to experience the struggles of desertion or destitution.

We were not perfect, but one would probably describe us as a model, middle class, black family, living without the struggles of survival when so many others were. We were a God-fearing family that possessed morals and values and were well known in the neighborhood and the City of Gary. As children, my siblings and I were dressed well and wore the best clothes money could buy. We never knew what lack was even during the depression years or when things were rationed during World War II.

Yes, you could say that as I was growing up, both my real father Walter, and Clisby, my stepfather, did very well. Everybody knew where we lived and knew about our family. We were the Robinsons in the little red  house with picture windows, a red wrought iron fence with a double yard and a huge flower garden right in the middle! We even had white wrought iron chairs to sit down outside the house! Yes, everybody knew the little house on Jefferson street. My mother always kept a good car that was never over 2 years old, even in the depression. Even though we lost our house, once they got out of the depression

2

years, they got their house back. Even my grandparents, everybody, got their own homes back. So, we lived well, even during the depression.

Although I don't remember much about that time, I do remember having one of the best Christmas's I ever had. Shirley Temple was extremely popular, and they came out with a Shirley Temple doll. That Christmas, I had the beautiful black Shirley Temple doll 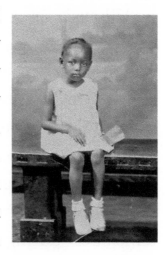 with beautiful black hair. I even had a buggy that was lined in satin! I was maybe about four or five and I remember that was a great Christmas. I think I even had a tricycle and didn't get another bike until I was a teenager. In fact, all of us had Schwinn's, which were the best bikes that money could buy. My sister and I shared a bedroom, and my brother had his own room, which was uncommon for a lot of families during that time. We were just fortunate to live really well, and we knew that we were blessed and highly favored by God.

Although my family was considered middle class, during the depression, we still experienced hardship and loss. Many people lost their homes, including us and we had to move in with my Great grandparents. There were a lot of us, but we were happy. During the Great Depression there was a lot of rationing. What I do remember during the depression, in fact, most of what I can remember, is what was told to me by my parents and grandparents. There was a lot of hunger. Men and women were lined up to receive aid from the city. Living in Gary, winters were hard and extremely cold. There were times, I was told, when men's ears would freeze off while they stood in line for food.

I remember hearing my parents talk about the anxiety, the fear, and the pain of seeing so many people suffer.

Seasons changed and our time for suffering was over. My parents were able to buy back our home and we continued to live well. Being young, I did not really know what was going on but, I do remember it being a joyous time in my life. Unfortunately, there were others around me that did not have what I had. I had friends that would come over to our house so they could eat, and we would play, but they did not have what I had. Their lack was not relevant to me at the time, but I did not mind sharing.

My grandfather, who we called Daddy Combs, always had a garden. As a result, we always had a lot of food and only had to worry about buying meat or other things you could not grow during the Great Depression.

I was always happy and enjoyed the little wagon ride into the garden during the summer with Daddy Combs. To me, riding in that little wagon was the best thing ever! When we got to our garden, my brother and I would play all through the sugar snap peas, in and around the tall okra, under the prickly cucumbers, and end up at the tomatoes. Then, we would grab a big warm juicy red tomato and sit under the rows of corn and eat them. Sometimes, we would even snatch a cucumber or whatever else we thought we could eat or liked to try. Daddy Combs let us run and get our fill of anything that we wanted. Then, he would load us back into the little wagon for the ride back home. We would always come home with a wagon full of stuff!

Season of Abundance, Bliss and Delight

My siblings and I were always guided to do our best in any situation, and to always push forward. This teaching became a great influence later in my life of difficulty. Church was a must every Sunday. When I say church, it was church all day! Sunday school, morning worship, youth meeting and then night service. The rule was if you are too sick for church, then you are too sick for any other activity during the week. This was a necessary prerequisite requirement we grew up with because there were always places we wanted to go throughout the week. So, going to church was a "no brainer"!

Our activities were what we enjoyed doing and we had no restrictions as long as they were wholesome, and my parents knew where we were at all times. We were the first to acquire most of all the latest  technology that came out on the market if we wanted it. We were the first to have a television when it hit the market. During the time I was growing up, they were hard to buy. We would encourage our friends and neighbors to come over to watch many events that appeared on television during that time like the Joe Louis fight since most did not have one.

As I reflect on my childhood and young adolescence, my life was enjoyable. My brother and I were very close and did a lot of things together. Every Saturday it was a regular thing to walk across Broadway which was the main center street in Gary that divided the West side of town where the streets were named after Presidents and, the East side of town where the streets were named after States. We would go to our Grandmother Comb's house who was always dressed and who would act surprised to see us. She would always give us a big smile, asking where we came from and where our money was. We would always respond that we were coming to go downtown with her, because we knew she had money in her stocking. She would always reach in her stocking and give each of us money to spend. Afterwards, we would go to town, shop, and eat at Goldblatt's, which was one of the largest department stores at the time with a cafeteria in the basement. We always made sure we left in enough time to get to the movies because Saturday was always movie day! There was not a Saturday that we did not see a movie unless the weather was really too bad for us to go. My brother and I went rink skating, bike riding and did many other activities together.

I grew up and lived life with one aunt, Verlon Grayson, who was my father's sister. She was a person that loved to party, lived the night life and all the trimmings and enjoyed life to the fullest. Most of her friends and associates were  male. However, she was very protective of me and my siblings and never wanted us to be exposed to her lifestyle or the friends she hung around. We could only visit if we called first and could never just "pop up" unannounced. She never had children of her own but two adopted daughters, Betty and Margo. Everybody called Aunt Verlon by her nickname, "Chick" because she worked in a chicken house. Her favorite pastime was making hot tamales which she became famous for in the neighborhood. She passed away at 85.

WALTER ROBINSON (DAD)

My father, Walter Robinson, was born to Janie Elberheart and Ab Combs. He had two sisters, Amos and Verlon. My father was the youngest and only son and the only one of the siblings that had children. I do not remember much about my father except that he was a very gentle, quiet man and a great dancer. My parents would go to formal dances every weekend. He worked in the steel mill and was also a fireman. My Father would always sit in the living room by the window in a big chair. He gave me one whipping when I was five years old during my birthday party. I was acting very ugly with my guests and he told me to stop. Of course, I did not. So, he took me in the room and turned me upside down, my dress fell over my head and he whipped me with his hand!

He died in 1939 when I was seven years old. At that time, medical science was not advanced enough to immediately diagnose a ruptured appendix and locked bowels. Additionally, people of color only had access to hospitals and doctors with limited medical knowledge and equipment. As I think of my father today, I still remember him as being a very kind and gracious man. I loved my father dearly and his passing was a hard thing to deal with as a child.

MARY RUTH (BROWN) ROBINSON WALKER ROBINSON (MOM)

Mary Ruth (Brown) Robinson, my mother, was born in 1903 in Augusta, Ga. to Emma and James Brown and was their only child. She was born when her mother was in her late forties and knew nothing of her relatives, because her mother was born in slavery. In 1913, my mother and grandmother moved to Evanston, IL after the death of her father and the threat of segregation in the South.

My mother was seven years old at the time. They later moved to Gary, Indiana in 1915, close to the steel mill and a culturally mixed area of town.

My mother grew up, met, and secretly married Walter Robinson. When the marriage was discovered by a nosey relative, they moved in together and had their first child that died at three  months old. After my sister Hardina was born in 1926, my parents built their first home with the money received from my grandmother's sale of her house and business in Georgia. This was my mother's dream home. My brother and I were born there.

After the death of my father in 1939, my mother became the primary supporter of our household. My mother, who was always taught to be industrious, found work in several places. She first started working at Slicks Laundry which, at that time, was the largest laundry facility in Gary. When World War II started, Kingsbury factory opened for men and women to make ammunition for the war. My mother worked in selective operations for the factory. Later, she became the first black female to drive a taxicab in the City of Gary.

During World War II, things began to change. There was rationing of gas, sugar, and many black outs occurred in the city. Bomb shelters were installed in many areas. Gary was considered a city of danger because, at that time, the largest steel mill in the United States and one of the largest oil refineries, Standard Oil located in East Chicago and Whiting, was within a twenty-mile radius of Gary. This resulted in many restrictions and air raids that occurred day or night. After D-Day was declared ending the war, the Kingsbury Factory closed about three months later. Things began to get back to normal.

Years passed, wounds healed, and when I was ten, my mother got remarried to a man named Clisby Walker. My sister, a teenager, wanted her to marry a flashier man just because he had a very nice-looking car! My mother of course was looking for a person who was a great provider, made good money, and could continue to keep us living in the comfortable lifestyle we were accustomed to. So, she married

Clisby Walker. I can truly say that he was the right person for us at the right time in our lives. They had two business ventures together. One, was on 23rd and Broadway with a street side stand selling a hot dog on a stick, known as a Pronto Pup. We now call it a Corn Dog. They were among the first to sell this hot dog on a stick dipped in a special formula batter, serving it with mustard or ketchup. The second was a store on 21st and Grant St., called Ruth Dairy Food Store. My stepdad was a great provider. He was blessed to have one of the best paying jobs in the Gary Steel Mill. In the forties, he was making thirty dollars an hour. We truly lived well and without turmoil.

In the midst of all the wonderful materials of life, there is something yet to learn. When you do not have to struggle for things, then you do not learn the true value of life and how to cope in the midst of adversity. We were taught independence, but yet robbed of putting it into practice. Not having to do without, taking things and life for granted, we never truly learned how to live in an unjust society.

Emma Brown Conner
(Mamma Conner)

E mma Brown Conner, my Grandmother who we called, "Mamma Conner" was born in the 18th century during the time of great slavery with no birth record or place of birth. She remembered that she was a "knee baby" when slavery ended. She also remembered her grandmother "Hanna" being a fighter of anybody who tried to whip her. According to Mamma Conner's information about the ending of slavery and being a "knee baby", they gave her a birth date of August 8, 1854. She married James Brown and had one child, Mary Ruth Brown, who was my mother. Even though she lived in the segregated South (Augusta Georgia), Mamma Conner had her own home and was an entrepreneur with a small business.

Mamma Conner always lived with us and dressed very old fashioned with long sleeves, long skirts and dresses. She was skeptical about modern appliances such as the refrigerator and would only use the old fashioned ice box with ice blocks. She was very private and even kept her closet locked. She loved to quilt, can fruits and vegetables, and go to church.

When walking to the neighborhood store, she would stop and talk to the "drunks" hanging around the liquor store and would always ask them when they were going to come to church. My siblings and I had so much fun bribing Mamma Conner to do our chores. We would get her to wash dishes by offering her either an ice cream cone, candy, or a quarter. But, at first, we would never pay her. After a while, she got clever on us and started demanding payment upfront!

Mamma Conner outlived all of her friends and began to feel so alone although we tried our best to cheer her up. She would just say that we did not understand. She lived to be 102 years old based on our calculated date of birth. When she passed away, her service was the first at our new church and everyone was so amazed to see most of the drunks she talked to in front of the liquor store walk in and attend her home going service.

RUTH HARDINA (MY OLDEST AND ONLY SISTER)

R uth Hardina was my oldest and only sister. She was named Ruth after our mother, but we called her Hardina. My parents lost our oldest sister, Beverly Romain when she was three months old, so, they were very happy when Hardina was born. Although Hardina was four and a half years older than me, we had a very good relationship. She was older, very active and

always had her head in a book. She was educational minded and concerned about the business side of life. Even as a child, she was always figuring things out, reading, and surveying the business world. Hardina was in so many activities and had so much talent! She sang with a group called The Robert Anderson singers from Chicago Illinois. She was a very good dancer and she spoke with eloquent diction and was very poised. She was just a different type of an individual and was always her own person. Hardina always carried herself with high integrity and character, she was tough and never lied even if she knew that she would get punished. She believed that it was always better to tell the truth even if it hurts. She was highly efficient in administrative skills, such as typing, shorthand and bookkeeping.

While working in church as a youth choir director, she rekindled a relationship with James Anderson who was in her high school graduating class. He had just returned home from the Army and had always been extremely fond of Hardina. They became engaged and in 1947, had one of the largest weddings at the largest African American church in the City of

Gary. Hardina was influential in assisting James in becoming the Senior Pastor of the First Church of God. He later founded the Brother's Keeper Homeless Shelter for men that is still operational today. Together, they build a legacy in the community and were well-respected and know throughout the city of Gary and surrounding areas.

Hardina and James became the first and only owners of a black religious bookstore, 'The Jesus Shoppe', in the City of Gary in the early 1970's and served most of the churches in the surrounding area for over 29 years. They carried Christian resources ranging from bibles, to tapes, to choir robes, to Sunday School lessons, to scarves and other gifts that could be either purchased in the store or ordered. The mobile bookstore traveled to church conventions and campgrounds across the country. Hardina was also known for organizing the first black booksellers' organization in many states that later became a chain known as (CAABA) Christian African American Booksellers Association.

I always loved being around my sister because I was so proud of her and she made me feel important. As we grew older in years, we spent more time together and I really cherished the moments we shared. Hardina and James were always humanitarians and so kind to others. They truly were the wind beneath my wings. It was my sister who encouraged me to move to Virginia with my children before she passed in the year 2000.

WALTER LAVERNE ROBINSON (BROTHER)

My brother, Walter LaVerne Robinson, and I were always close. Since we were only two years apart, I would follow him almost everywhere. He grew to be a tall, slim and very handsome teenager. He was a very immaculate dresser and had remarkable musical talent. He was popular in school and played several instruments but excelled the greatest on piano and flute. Walter became the head drum major for Roosevelt High School Marching Band which was a high-profile position and major accomplishment during that time.

Walter started having seizures at a young age that continued until he was fifteen. Although they would only last for a minute or two, someone needed to be around him to make sure he did not hurt himself if he fell. This would irritate my sister and me because he took advantage of his condition by always using the bathroom first or making us wait on him while he took his time to look perfect! Walter was fancy, a very elaborate dresser and always strived to look his best. Because my parents were "well off", he was able to get the clothes he wanted to wear. I can say that he was a person focused on his image. Once when it was freezing outside, and we were walking to school. A man pulled up and offered us a ride. The man's car was coated with rust and had a loud muffler. I started to get in, but Walter pulled me back and said, "No thank you." I turned to him and said "Why did you do that? I am freezing!" He looked at me and simply stated, "Emily, a proud walk is better than a poor ride any day."

Walter was a person that was not afraid of anything, unlike me. So, it made it easy for him to always scare me. I remember once, going over to my grandmother's house, and as we were crossing Broadway which is divided between the North and South side, he picked up this snake and he just dangled it in my face. I was so scared that I ran all the way home, bursting into the door and almost knocking my grandmother down. I was out of breath and she said, "what's wrong" and I could only say, "Jr., Jr., Jr., scared me!". Then he came in, and he was so tickled, he was just laughing, and he held up the snake and dangled it saying, "see, it's just a dead snake!" My grandmother said, "Well you just come in here and I am going to give you a whipping because you are always scaring this girl ". There were several incidents involving me and Walter having what he considered "fun." At one point, he wanted to be a mortician. He loved to go into the funeral parlor and would always con me into going with him. He would stroll in and ask the mortician, "Do you have anybody dead in here today?" So, they would tell us which room to go into, and so on. He would tell me not to look but get me interested in the beautiful flower bouquets surrounding the casket. I would turn my attention to reading the names on the name tags out loud being unaware that he had slowly moved to the door. Then, as I would be standing in front of the casket by myself, he would softly call to me. "Emily, Emily... look at that person rising up or their mouth or eyes are beginning to open!" My imagination would go wild, and I could see the person's mouth or eyes open or, they were actually getting up! And when I looked around, I would be the only one in the room with the dead person. I would get tee-totally frantic, tearing up flowers as I ran out. He would be outside just laughing his heart out. The last time he ever scared me in a funeral parlor, I tore up the flowers, knocked Walter over and the man came running. I was outside on the sidewalk screaming "Junior did it, Junior did it!" In spite of all that, he was a lot of fun.

Walter was a natural musician, and nobody really knew he could actually play as well as he did. My sister, Hardina, was taking lessons and she hated them and never wanted to practice. One day, we came in and Walter was sitting at the piano and he was just playing. My mother said, "WOW, how did you learn to play?" He shrugged his shoulders and said, "I don't know, I just can do it." He started lessons and outgrew all of the music instructors in the area by the time he was 16 years old and was considered a young Beethoven. He gave a concert at the largest Methodist church in Gary and received a standing ovation for performing the 'Warsaw Concerto'. Walter played the flute, clarinet, and alto saxophone and his favorite music was the Blues. Prior to his death, Walter's plan was to study music at The Music Conservatory of Chicago.

At seventeen, due to severe kidney issues, Walter could not attend school for an entire year and was taught by a bedside teacher. His faith increased remarkably during that time and he simply believed God would heal him. He refused to take any medicine and over time, became worse to the point of death. One Sunday night Dr. Benjamin Grant came to the house, looked at him, shook his head and said, "He is dying, and I might as well sit down because before I go a block, I will have to turn around." After about fifteen or twenty minutes, my brother called out for my mother. When she opened the door, he was sitting up in bed looking like he had never been sick. The entire bed was covered with a reddish orange substance. He told her he was hungry. My mother cooked him a complete meal and he ate all of it without difficulty. Over the last several weeks, he had eaten very little.

God allows some things in our lives to humble us and to show others his glory. Dr. Grant became a minister shortly after seeing my brother healed. God answered Walter's prayer with complete healing, the ability to go back to school, and to graduate with a different attitude about life. He lived free of any ailments until February 1949, my senior year in high school. Walter, at this point in his life, had the faith of a mustard seed; proving that faithfulness and standing on the Word of God works.

God is a great God, and He does miraculous things in our life. But, when we go back to our past ways, we are saying, "God, I can take it from here." and not really accepting what He has done and the plans He has for our future.

Walter was well, up and running, as one might say. He had no worries and made big plans to go to the Chicago Music Conservatory to become an important figure in the music industry. He had a good job, doing his thing as we all say. He became ill, not hurting, with a cough that would not let him maintain food or water in his body. I believe he felt what was about to happen. He was quiet for three days, went to work and back home, having little to say to anyone. This was an unusual difference from a person who had some place to go every night of the week. I recall my mother asking him what hurt him. He simply stated, "not   hing, I just can't keep anything in my stomach". On Saturday morning February 8th, he asked to go to the hospital. I know now that he did not want to be home when God received him from this life on February 9, 1949.

This reminds us that the years are so short, we should be grateful for the time spent with each other and that time is so important because it always ends.

EMILY JANET ROBINSON COOPWOOD

As a child, I had a quiet nature and did not express my hurts or true feelings about things. I would hold things in regardless of how bad I might be wounded internally by what was said or done to me. However, I was always concerned about what others thought and I cared deeply about their feelings, never wanting to see them hurt.

As an adolescent, my personality changed, and I became more carefree in spirit. I loved life and all it had to offer! I enjoyed having fun, going places and doing things I'd never done before. I loved to talk to people and sometimes had a tendency to talk too much and say exactly what was on my mind. Because I enjoyed interacting with people, I started selling things to make extra money growing up. My mother, who was a great cook, would make doughnuts and bake mini pies for me to sell in our neighborhood every Saturday afternoon. I would sell magazines and newspapers to local businesspeople.

My most defining character trait growing up was being naive. I trusted, believed and took people at their word with no questions asked. I grew up in a home where telling the truth and knowing that someone would keep their word, was a primary belief. My parents were always truthful even down to punishment for wrongdoing they promised to give at a later time! As a result, I grew up trusting what a person said regardless of what I saw, and I never worried about the "what if".

In high school, I had a small circle of friends I loved dearly. We walked to school, came home to my house for lunch most days and hung out together after school. My home was my friend's favorite hangout because my mother always made them feel special and welcomed. She would have snacks available and allowed us to play music and dance in the basement. Sometimes, she would let us decorate the basement according to the holidays.

In high school, I was a member of the Girls Athletic Association known as the GAA which was an elite girls club that required good grades, participating in at least two sports and the ability to swim. My sports were volleyball, speedball, track and swimming. I was also a member of

the Mixed Chorus in 1949 when we introduced the new Roosevelt High School theme song that they used until the school closed in Gary. I played the violin in the Orchestra, had a short tenure of playing the trumpet in the band, and attended most of the school sponsored activities including the senior prom. I participated in all the popular clubs and activities in high school and was always the best dressed most days. I attended church regularly, participated in most youth activities, loved going to Riverview Amusement Park in Chicago and went to West Middlesex, Pennsylvania Church of God Camp every summer. One could say that I lived a carefree and fun life until graduating high school.

Although I lived life with good parents who provided very well for me and my siblings, I always had a heart to help others, especially children. Every time I saw someone with a baby, I would ask to hold them. This feeling later cultivated into my desire to become a nurse and a mother.

There were two defining moments that occurred during my last year in high school. One, my greatest honor at that time in my life, was being the Maid of Honor at my sister's wedding. Secondly, first of many sad life changing events, my brother who was my best friend, passed away in 1949 at the age of 19.

As the only sibling at home, I began to experience a turning point in my life. My sister was now married and living in another town and my brother, my best friend, had passed away. This all happened in February 1949, the year I was to graduate from Roosevelt High School. After graduation, I worked in Chicago at Montgomery Wards with plans to attend college for nursing.

Little did I know that I would soon learn by my own choice, all that we are comes from God and when we lose our identity, we lose who we are in Christ.

Humbleness leads to obedience.

It is only when we learn who we are, that we are not characterized by someone else's description of us.

It took many years of me learning how not to be manipulated by the actions and feelings of others that were especially close to me, to finally be free.

Unknown Preparation

Growing up in a Christian environment, as a child and in my early teens, I would attend a national church convention in a huge rural underdeveloped place in West Middlesex, PA in August, during the hottest time of the summer. This place was a totally different view from my normal lifestyle. We pumped water for every occasion from eating to bathing to cleaning. Everyone slept in huge wooden buildings with large rooms that held ten to twelve little cotton cots for people to sleep on. I had my first experience with going to a place called the "Outhouse" to use the restroom. It was far back in the woods, so you dare not go out at night by yourself.

As a child, it was fun and different because we could also escape the eyes of our mother or grandmother who spent most of their time in the big tent tabernacle singing and worshipping God. The tent, with no windows for ventilation, held about 400 people. It had a straw floor and hard wooden benches to sit on. There were lights strung up around the main areas of the grounds where most of the people congregated. The big kitchen area where everyone ate three meals each day, was located right under the big sleeping area. I remember the campgrounds being the same for many of my younger years. Until one year, I returned, and things had changed and continued to do so after that time.

Little did I know that the humbling experiences I went through during the years of going to the campgrounds, would someday be re-experienced through the man I would later marry. A man, because of his own life story and struggles as a child, would not see that the life he was providing for his family was impoverished.

THEODORE ROOSEVELT COOPWOOD JR. (MY HUSBAND OF 67 YEARS)

Theodore Roosevelt Coopwood Jr., was born in Parken, Arkansas on November 10, 1926 to Liller Ann and Theodore Roosevelt Coopwood Sr. Theodore, Ted or Big Coop as many would call him, always desired to give people a fair, honest and supportive hand in any situation they were encountering. He strived to be the answer to life's problems for the poor in spirit, those in need of assistance, advice, and general safety.

As a child, Ted or Junior as he was called then, left Parken, Arkansas when his parents married and moved to a large

Italian community in Chicago Heights, IL where there was much prejudice against blacks. Because he was from the South, the children viewed him as an outsider, assumed he could not read, attempted to fight him, and take his lunch on a daily basis. So, he had to defend himself almost continuously. However, because he was larger than most of the kids, he was able to fight them off going to and from school each day.

The most vivid memory Ted had as a child was when his father took them to Ottawa, MI and left them to live in an isolated wooded area while he went to preach. The house was so ragged that they covered the inside of the house with newspaper to shield the holes and to keep out the sun and weather. He had to walk a mile to school but before going to school, he had to go hunt for rabbits or squirrels and sometimes fish to make sure there was food to eat. There was a time when there was no food and his mother actually cooked oak leaves off the trees for food to eat. Ted remembers being so hungry that he would stare at a billboard food advertising and get full! As a result of Ted's impoverished life as a child, he was always sensitive to people who were hungry or needed the basic life necessities.

Much of Ted's drive and motivation came from growing up in an impoverished lifestyle all of his life. He grew up having little to no food to eat on most days and living in condemnable housing conditions. His home environment was stressful because his father walked away, leaving him as the oldest child and son at a young age, to care for his mother and younger brothers. These conditions caused him to begin work as a young child which greatly hampered his education and normal childhood development. As a result of not being able to function well academically, his peers and some teachers labeled him as slow and incapable of learning.

Because Ted was the primary support for his mother and brothers throughout his adolescent years, he needed to work jobs that were normally reserved for grown men such as construction, railroad, and the steel mill. His large build and unordinary strength as a young teenager afforded him those opportunities because age verification credentials were not required in the late 30's and early 40's.

Struggling to survive is how Ted lived most of his life. Even when he worked and made a respectable salary, the struggle to survive was always emotionally present.

This entry from the steel city of Gary represented the Gary, Ind. Post Tribune in the Golden Gloves Tournament of Champions. Front row, left to right: John Reid Thomson, 112 pounds; Joseph L. Woodard, 118 pounds; Roy Joiner, 126 pounds; Albert LaBroi, 135 pounds. Back row: Roy Terry, 175 pounds; Pete T'omson, 147 pounds; Thae were Coopwood, heavy weight. Allen Douglas, 160 pounds, was absent.

He lived with the feelings of rejection growing up as a child and even into adulthood, believing that he had to prove his worth even to his parents. In high school, Ted struggled to be in school during the day and work at night. However, he still managed to play football, his favorite sport and he boxed to keep himself physically fit and strong.

At the age of 18 and a senior in high school, Ted was drafted into the Army when World War II started like most of the boys during that time. This robbed him of the first major accomplishment he would have experienced in his life. In 1944, the Army environment was extremely disciplined, controlled, and racism was prevalent. Ted's ability to fight, his physical strength and ability to articulate well gave him a great advantage over other soldiers, even white soldiers.

As Ted grew up, his father, although absent most of the time, blamed him for anything that happened to his siblings and any trouble they got into because he was the oldest. His mother had very little confidence in him, made him work all his childhood life and controlled all the money he made until he left home at age 22. Even after he came back from the military and purchased a house and fully furnished it for his mother to live in, her treatment towards him did not change. All of his mother's life, Ted tried to show how much he loved her by doing everything he could and finally, prior to her death, she said, "Junior, you are a good boy." She died holding his hand.

Although Ted's entire life was hard and frayed, he went to church and maintained a great respect and reverence for God. He believed that he could do anything with God as the source of his strength. One of his favorite Bible Scriptures was Psalm 144:1, "Blessed be the LORD my strength, which teacheth my hands to war, and my fingers to fight." He would also quote Philippians 4:13, "I can do all things through Christ who strengthens me".

He always felt that he had to prove himself and who he was to everyone by demonstrating great strength. Every time he met a man, he would grip their hand so tight that it would bring them to their knees. He gloated when they said, "Coopwood, you got a strong handshake!".

This to him was delivering a non-verbal message that he was in charge and don't mess with me!

Ted would always say, "He that does not hustle, will not have, and he that has, must hustle to keep". This quote summed up how he lived his life, what he believed and why he continued to fight when others quit.

Ted was the Golden Glove Heavyweight Champion for the North Central US for several years. He was a spiring partner for Eza Charles. He was Grievance representative for Inland Steel Galvanize and a personal friend of Governor Roger Branigin of Indiana. Ted received a personal invitation to President Lindon Johnson's Inauguration. He was a Judo and Athletic

Instructor in both the Army and the Marines. He had the honor of meeting Jesse Owens, the fastest running man in the Olympics, Joe Lewis, the World Heavyweight Boxer and Jackie Robinson. He was Vice President of the Lake County Youth Society and was invited to speak at First Church of God where I attended church as a Sophomore in high school.

Journey Begins

After my brother's death and five months before my high school graduation, I recall seeing Theodore at church. He was a poised and motivated speaker that captured the audience as he spoke. However, I never thought that I would actually see him again since he was more my sister's age and not mine. As I was crossing Broadway walking home from my Grandmother Comb's house, Theodore came up to me and started a conversation. Immediately, my introduction was, "Hello, are you looking for my sister and her husband?". He was a perfect gentleman, stating, "No" and he continued to walk me home. Of course, it was ok, because I knew him to be a young man of Christian character and our conversation was about church and family. After Theodore left and I went inside, I told my mother about meeting him and our conversation. She was elated because she remembered him from Church and asked if I had invited him to an upcoming church performance at the high school. I said no but looked for his number to invite him. This invitation was the beginning of a whirlwind of events in my life, which I had no way of expecting.

After the invitation to the church event, the relationship with Theodore became one of gradual possession and control, which I did not perceive or recognize for years to come. My exposure to people impacted by a life of rejection and insecurity was more than lacking. I had none and even though God gave numerous signs, I did not and could not receive them because of my lack of knowledge and understanding.

Theodore, even though he loved God, talked about God, and carried a bible daily, was insecure.

Theodore portrayed great confidence and it caused me to believe that everything he said was right and truthful. He had so much experience for his age, and I had none. And since I left God out of the equation, I really messed up. So, I like Eve, bit the apple!

My life quickly became more entangled with Theodore's because he was always around. He became so confident of himself and what he wanted, that he never asked my parents for their permission or approval to marry me until the Christmas after my graduation when he gave me a vanity set engraved with the initials "EC" already on it along with an engagement ring. He demonstrated, yet again, a spirit of control and manipulation that I could not and did not want to see.

So, I got lost in the blissful relationship, even though it was not what I truly desired at the time. My original focus was on going to college until Theodore came into my life and quickly convinced me to go in the opposite direction. If I would have taken time to observe, not just what I saw, but the character traits displayed, reactions to certain situations or just the attitude about daily life occurrences, I probably would have made a different choice.

Everything that talks and truly looks good is not a gift or even what is planned for us; we are often tempted by emotions; we forget that the choices we make in life all have consequences

What we fail to see about life is that God's providence is tied to time, and He is the God of interaction in our most needed circumstances and uncomfortable situations.

On April 14, 1950, I made the choice to marry Theodore Roosevelt Coopwood, Jr. I again succumbed to his wishes and we married in my pastor's home instead of having a wedding like my parents wanted for me. Allowing my parents to give me a wedding would have taken the control away from him since the Mother of the Bride and the Bride controls most of what occurs in the preparation process. This also robbed my parents of the celebration with friends and family since they were very well known in Gary.

I pause here to say to every young lady who is planning to get married. Never rob yourself of the greatest gift and pleasure God gives of having your father's blessing of presenting you to your soul mate as you pass from one protective covering to the other; granting you blessing as you change your name to your husband's name. This is not just for your lasting remembrance but your parents as well.

Now married to a man who grew up as a child feeling the burdens of being the oldest son and responsible for the welfare of his siblings and his mother, my life's journey into the unknown had begun.

Words spoken in fear seem to paralyze the mind into a remembrance that one cannot forget. What we cannot escape, we must develop a battle plan to overcome it.

TOUR OF DUTY

Within nine months of our marriage, my husband (Ted) was redrafted into the Marines. It was mandatory at that time to be in the reserves for any emergency after being discharged from the army. He chose the Marines because, at that time, black soldiers were not a part of that branch of service, and he felt he would not be called. However, his experience in the Army made him a priority. He was a Hand-to-Hand Combat, Judo and Athletic Instructor and they needed him to train soldiers for the Korean War. This assignment made him even more aggressive.

The extreme prejudice in the Marine Corps made Ted's time very difficult. There were only two black men in the entire regiment. Ted's dominant character, size, strength, and combat technique abilities were known and made him a constant target. However, these attributes allowed him to successfully complete basic training on Parris Island, SC. Ted and the other black soldiers were separated after basic training from their regiment and sent to Camp Lejeune, NC. It was there that Ted was intentionally wounded while playing football. He was admitted into the hospital after being spiked in the left knee and he developed blood clots in his leg. Ted, although the Marines initially refused to grant because of his status and experience, petitioned the appropriate officials and received an honorable discharge and a disability pension. After the discharge from the Marines, Ted gradually became more dominant and controlling.

SIBLING SUPPORT

When Ted was discharged from the military, we had been married for almost three years and had no children. My sister, Hardina, who had married several years before me, lived in another city in Indiana with four small children very close in age and a fifth one on the way. Her husband, James, was a minister, going to school at the time and had very little time to assist her with the children. Needless to say, my sister was traumatized, overwhelmed, and needed help. Since I had no children at the time, I volunteered to keep her only daughter, Beverly, until after the baby was born. She dropped her off and Ted and I kept her for almost a year.

Between 1950 through 1965, for some reason, people with children were not welcomed in rental property. Ted and I had just come back from Carolina and were renting a furnished basement apartment when Beverly came to stay with us. Initially, the landlord was agreeable with us having her but after a few months, became annoyed with an infant being in the apartment and began to constantly complain. We decided to look for another place to live. Unfortunately, we were rejected when we would say we had no children and then they would see Beverly in the car. In desperation, Ted found an advertisement in the paper for a house to rent or buy. The house had all inside facilities, a furnace and was ready to occupy. We made our move with my niece to that area. This was the beginning of my experience of living in a place called Small Farms.

Although this was the only housing we could find at the time, the move to the house in Small Farms caused a lot of friction with my family. My mother and Aunt Verlon came to see where we were living and were upset because they knew this was not the lifestyle I was accustomed to and they felt it was all Ted's idea. What they did not realize, and I didn't tell them, was that I accepted the move because we had no other place to go. My sister came and got her daughter two months after her fifth baby was born.

STILL BORN

Ted and I had now been married four years which was a total surprise we even lasted that long. After a short stay in New York, we moved back to Indiana into the home we originally had in Small Farms. The house was not big but really nice inside with two bedrooms, one bath, kitchen, living room with a floor furnace and running hot and cold water. We had a large backyard that was decent for the area we lived in.

During my first pregnancy, there was a lot of controversy because Ted was dead set on having boys and could not perceive the idea that the baby could be anything else. He was so adamant that he refused to paint the room or make plans for anything other than a male baby. I believe this was due to his lack of communication with his mother and deep resentments against anything female. He was further mentally warped by reading specific scriptures in Proverbs and taking the passages pertaining to women completely out of context. At times, he became so irritated about the issue that he made radical statements that left feelings of remorse later in his life. Unfortunately, he did not recognize the sovereignty of God and His control over our lives whether seen or unseen. Our child, that I carried for nine months without difficulty until it was time to deliver, was a "still born" girl that weighed nine pounds and was as beautiful as ever. Ted was heartbroken because the child that he didn't want, he now wanted but didn't have.

Now God is still waiting for a reform. We are not our own. It is God that gives life according to his way and takes it according to His pleasure, and He does it in His timing.

After my recovery from the delivery of my first child, I decided to go to nursing school at a Catholic institution in Gary, my hometown. Although I passed their entrance exam, they refused to allow me in because I was married. Students attending the school were  required to stay in the facility housing which was off limits to males and married students could not have their husbands visit. They recommended I enroll at Purdue University Hammond Campus, which had an intense program for Licensed Practical Nurse (LPN), and I would be able to commute daily. I was accepted and received my diploma of graduation in 1956. I took and passed the state board examination for my LPN license, obtained a certificate in Pharmacology, and began working at Methodist Hospital in the Obstetrical Department.

FIRST AWAKENING

While I was attending school, I had an opportunity to help a person who I considered a close and trusted friend. She was also in a controlling marriage but left and needed temporary shelter for her and her three children. Since Ted and I had no children at the time and we had an extra bedroom, I agreed to help and let her move in until she was able to move on. Because I was a person who took things at face value, believing, trusting, and never looking for wrong in people, I did not see the pattern and what she began to do right under my nose. She knew when I was at school or worked and when my husband worked. She was truly a schemer, and I had no knowledge of it until it became a major conflict and Ted brought it to my attention. After several days of observing her actions and attitude, I decided to approach her with what I observed. She was eager to say to me that she did not succeed in her efforts to destroy my marriage. This ended many years of what I thought was a sincere friendship, one that went from grade school through high school. After she left, I refused to harbor hate against her and still regarded her as a special acquaintance. This was my first awakening and lesson on not taking people for granted and learning how to observe a person's attitude and character.

BUS DESEGREGATION

Ted became the 2nd Negro bus driver hired in the city of Gary in 1958. He drove the city bus during a period of legal racial segregation and there were housing boundaries for the Negroes, Latino, and Whites. Gary was a booming steel mill town and had a section called steel mill quarters where immigrants who work in the mills lived. The three black drivers, including Ted, were assigned to the white areas of the city which made the job very stressful. However, Ted was very defensive and unafraid. He became so well known until black people would wait for his bus just because he would let them sit in the front of the bus. He would also pass up stops to get them to work on time.

Ted, after some time, became a problem for the bus company because he would confront any white person that made a racial remark to him directly or while on his bus. He would immediately stop the bus, go back and actually demand an apology or challenge them outside the bus. Ted believed that he had to either outthink the white man to get ahead or fight. Unfortunately, this misguided character trait cost him, and he resigned from the bus company.

We must decide to see ourselves as God sees us. We are not bond slaves of man only to Jesus Christ who gives us true identity. The paralysis of refusing to act leaves you where you are, and you can go no further. Once you act, you are never the same. Everything becomes an extension of the past, a contrast of the future, and a link to God and His power.

THE STRUGGLE AND
NOW, CHILDREN

I n 1958, after eight years of marriage, the challenge of parenthood began. We had many ups and downs by this time. We were still living in Small Farms, I was now working full-time in the hospital and Ted was doing construction jobs, landscaping lawns, and hauling dirt to various homes for lawn restoration and upkeep. He had also taken on several political endeavors. Because of Ted's dedication to God, he began to fight against several roadhouses of illicit nature that catered to the wealthy and prominent citizens of Gary. They would come into the Small Farms community at night to gamble and fulfill their sexual desires with women brought in by the roadhouses. This endeavor became an obsession for Ted, and he was determined to close all of them and clean up the community. The battle became so tense that we began to get threats and one day when I was away with the baby and Ted was at work, our house was burned down, and we lost everything.

As a result of the fire, we relocated back into the city of Gary and lived there for almost five years. After moving back into the city, I became pregnant with my second child, which was another girl. May I add by this time my husband had realized God is in control of life and does as He sees fit. He will challenge us to accept His will for our lives regardless of how we feel or think. He is God of all creation. He only gives life, male or female.

Now with three children and my second child, who was five, ready to attend Kindergarten, Ted decides to move back to

Small Farms. The house we were living in at the time was going to be sold. So, Ted decided to renovate a little house located at the back of the lot we owned into living quarters.

I wanted my children to attend school in the Gary school system and not in the Small Farms. The system in Small Farms was part of Calumet Township and all of the blacks and most of the poorer class of white people who lived in trailers went to an elementary school called Black Oak. Since I was not familiar with this system, I felt my children would be deprived of the education I wanted them to have. I succeeded with my first child attending Kindergarten in the Gary school system and was about to enroll my second child using the address of our previous home. This plan was exposed by our six-year-old daughter who was very intelligent. One day she was not picked up on time and when her teacher asked why she could not walk home but had to wait to be picked up, she told her that she could not cross the highway to go home. This was when the Small Farms was divided by I-94 and a bridge was under construction to connect the two sections. As a result of the inquiry, she was automatically transferred to the Black Oak school district.

LIFE IN SMALL FARMS – 66 YEARS

S mall Farms, a rural area outside of the City of Gary, well water, septic tanks, poor roads, and a community with some of the poorest people I had ever seen. A place I would have never imagined I would end up living and raising my children.

Life in the Small Farms came with many struggles, challenges, and lack of many of the basic necessities for living. We moved back to the Small Farms permanently and lived in the little pieced together house located in the back of the lot we owned with four small children, two girls and two boys. It had two bedrooms, a small living room that ran into the dining area, a bathroom with no connected toilet, sink or tub and a cutout area where the stove and refrigerator were located.

Prior to us moving back to the Small Farms, Ted was hired by Inland Steel Mills in the Galvanize department. As a result of his aggressive nature and the ability to articulate well, he won the election in his department for Grievance Arbitrator. He worked to get better working conditions in the Galvanize department and fought to get more black men hired. He was so committed to his position and making positive changes, that he would visit the president of Inland Steel Mill in his office in Chicago, IL. Ted's efforts to represent and speak on behalf of other workers caused him to be well known throughout the company.

Soon after we moved to the Small Farms, Ted was asked to run for Precinct Committeeman to represent the community in the county political arena.

This position fed Ted's strong passion to help all the people in the community. His first mission was to close all roadhouses and gambling joints in the community to make it safer for his children and the children in the community. This endeavor came with much resistance from those benefiting from the illicit activity. Ted was set up and incarcerated as a result of a lady who was bribed with money from a prominent lawyer, to lie about circumstances that never occurred. However, the Governor of Indiana who was a personal friend of Ted's and knew the type of man he was and what he was trying to do for the community, gave him a governor's pardon. Ted was released and his record was expunged.

Many changes occurred during Ted's tenure as Precinct Committeeman for the Small Farms community. Remembering the injustices and prejudices he endured in his own life, he was an advocate for justice, and at times, dogmatic in his attempt to get things done for others. All the roadhouses and gambling places were eventually closed down. Streetlights were installed on the corners of major road crossings, gravel roads with large potholes were paved and schools were integrated. As a member of the school board, he demanded the Calumet Township school system be integrated by hiring black teachers in each of the five schools in the district. One of the first black female teachers to be hired at Calumet High School was a highly rated English teacher. She was an advocate and mentor for all of my children and those in the community until she retired.

Ted, when he spoke with that deep and loud voice, would get the attention of everyone in the room. He knew and was respected by governors, senators, congressmen, mayors and many prominent people, not only in Gary, but throughout the State of Indiana and Chicago, IL area.

As a result of his successful fight against crime and corruption in the Small Farms, Theodore Coopwood became a legend in the community and state as an advocate for justice, and the welfare for the needy.

UNCONDITIONAL LOVE
DEMONSTRATED

My life with Ted was a journey of learning experiences. I not only learned what it was like to live in hard times, but how to genuinely help others in need. The life we lived taught my children how to appreciate and accept all people regardless of race or nationality. I fed and housed many people, but my greatest test of love was during a severe Chicago blizzard of 1967 and the northwest was paralyzed. There were tractor trailer trucks and cars stranded on I-94 right behind our little house. Many people had to seek refuge in houses in our community. An entire family of four who were of a different nationality had to stay with us for an entire week. This was a great experience in seeing as well as getting to know people for who they are. I obtained a deeper awareness that no man is different from another and we all have to help one another. Ted, our young boys, and several of the men in the community took sleds and made a pathway to the highway to empty produce trucks. The truckers were stranded, and they decided to distribute the food to the people in the community instead of letting it perish. This demonstrated that we are really one big family and God is the father and source of all of us.

Sunday, March 8, 1992

● **Community** ●

'ed Coopwood leads fight

community leader describes his beliefs, motivating principles

dy Banks
oondent

(Y — Theodore "Ted" Coopaas been leading a fight for a in a community he believes most integrated area in the

ple are of a common trend he said of the many farmers in iall Farms area in Calumet hip. "We get along well with al incidents."

many years, Coopwood has lumet Township in his best inus a citizen, precinct committeed local leader.

10 years, he served as a capthe Calumet Township Preirganization, before Calumet hip became a part of Gary. today, his relentless effort to sanitary water for some areas district, because of polluted Sandy Joe, still has him g.

ive been trying to get water all Farms and some other arce the mid-1950s, and yet we ve the same well water we had before I even came here in ie said.

wood, who has served as precommitteeman for G3-1 from 80 and from 1984 to the pres-

Theodore Coopwood

ent, is also trying to obtain city lighting and fair snow removal.

"When it snows, they seem to make one street in this area a priority and that's it," he said.

Coopwood has lived in the Small Farms area for 40 years. During that time he has fought to get paved roads and was a volunteer troubleshooter in the effort to prevent Calumet High School from becoming state

property in the mid-1970s.

He believes the Lake Ridge School system is the most integrated school system in the area.

Lake Ridge School Superintendent Nick G. Julius said the system has about 3,000 students — 11 percent blacks and 11 percent Hispanics.

Julius said the system has an integrated professional, non-professional and administrative staff as well.

Coopwood and his wife, Emily, reared their six children in the Lake Ridge school system, and he said he is proud of it. He said he is also proud of who he is, where he lives and the faith they have that keeps them going.

The retired steelworker said he has been able to help his community because there has always been a need for leadership.

He describes a leader as "someone who is unequal in love, passionate for all people, believes in the real God and fairness for every people or person regardless of the occasion. He said a leader stands firm in what he believes in and dominates the ground which he covers and that his word is his bond.

Leadership is a skill the precinct committeeman has developed

throughout his life. He worked on a railroad at the age of 14, worked in the mill at 16, served as a construction foreman in the Army in 1945, served in the Marines in 1951, and was one of the youngest blacks hired as a bus driver for Gary Transit in 1954 at age 23.

In 1958-60, he studied metallurgics at Purdue University Calumet and economics at St. Joseph's College now Calumet College. He obtained an associate degree in labor education/arbitration from Roosevelt College (now Roosevelt University) in Chicago while working at the mill and attending night school.

At 65, the community leader said he has learned to fight for what he believes in. "My parents taught me from the Bible to fear God and not to fear man," he said. His minister father brought him to Gary in 1936.

Coopwood, who was born in Parken, Ark., said politics and church are strong forces in this world, but God's power is second to none.

The community leader said he has always has the spiritual power and believes "He that does not hustle does not have . . . And he that has must hustle to keep it."

As a leader in Calumet Township he continues to hustle for his community.

96

BREAKING POINT

After fifteen years working at Inland Steel Mill, one of the foreman Ted worked with began to antagonize him and caused work to become very stressful. This caused internal turmoil and bothered Ted's spirit on a daily basis. He was one to handle pressure well and always had a defensive nature. Little did this foreman know that his deliberate actions against Ted were about to cause an explosion, and Ted would not care who got hurt. The day of reckoning came. The foreman demanded Ted to do a task in a disrespectful tone. The foreman, before he could react, immediately found himself hurled across the room like a dishrag. This was an upsetting incident, but the pressure had been building up inside of Ted for months. As a result of Ted's action, he was suspended and eventually dismissed from his job. Fortunately, during arbitration, they granted him a pension based on his years of service and all he had done for others while employed.

THE HUSTLE

After Ted lost his job at the Inland Steel Mill, he decided to start his own company, Ted's Maintenance Construction Co. This endeavor resulted in him having more time as Precinct Committeeman to help people with a variety of needs. He would start working early each day and did not come home until late. However, he always made time to be at the children's events. Being present at their activities was a big deal for Ted because his parents attended none of the school sports or other activities he participated in while in school. This left a deep emotional scar which made him determined to never miss anything his children were in. We were always there.

With the company and committeeman responsibilities, much of Ted's time was dedicated to people in the Small Farms community, their needs, and concerns. This left me to always figure out the needs and schemes of making things work for the entire family. Since I did not want to leave my children unattended and be available to attend their school activities, I worked in the Calumet School system during the weekdays and at the hospital as a nurse on the weekends. Unfortunately, Ted made working very stressful for me because he felt, as the man of the house, he should be in control of all resources. We had so many disagreements over money and it led me to do things I should not have done. My attitude during that time caused me to move away from Godly principles as well as my own personal principles.

OUR CHILDREN

Now, with three boys and three girls, Ted was still always busy. However, the children were his pride and joy. It was not that Ted did not want a comfortable and peaceful home environment, he just had never experienced it himself. He did not understand the importance of children feeling safe and having certain things while growing up. I came to realize that a person can never know what a different lifestyle entails if they have never been exposed to it. Ted and my lifestyles were so vastly different growing up and that created conflict in many areas in our life and the lives of our children.

Our six children were always my main concern. They grew up with meager beginnings, along with mental and sometimes physical abuse. On several occasions, the conditions for me and the children would become too much, and we would leave. God would always heal my heart and give me strength to return and start again. Starting again was not my idea, but God knew my heart and I always wanted my children to grow up with both parents. I truly believed that all children need both parents because each one has unique guidance and contributions designed by God for their lives. Ted had many words of great wisdom that benefited those who listened to him. However, although he gave great advice to others, he found difficulty in applying what he knew or finding the right method to instruct and encourage himself and his family.

In 1974, once again I decided that I had enough of the conflict and struggles. I found a house to buy in the Gary Tolliston District. Although the house was a comfortable home with everything I had asked God for, I was not really satisfied. My three boys did not want to move but remained with their dad in Small Farms. My girls were excited to finally live, so they thought, in a decent environment. I managed to work two full-time jobs, the school system during the day and nursing at the hospital at night. My schedule still allowed me time to meet the needs of my children and attend activities. I had no problems with the girls doing what they were supposed to do. I thought the setup was ideal until resentment started flaring up between the siblings. The boys were suffering with their dad and the girls did not care. This I could not have because they were all my children, and all had my love and devotion.

The crucial turning point came around Christmas time that year. I made up my mind that there would be no division among my children even if I had to sacrifice myself for all of them. I decided to let the house go, move back to the wilderness of Small Farms, and make a home for all of my family, whether they appreciated it or not. My girls thought I was weak and had lost my mind by giving up the conveniences to go back to nothing. God gave me the strength and I invested all the money I had into fixing up the house to make it one of the best Christmases ever. I learned that when the Spirit of God guides us, our personal ambitions seem to become insignificant.

Sometimes the multitude of experiences God allows us to go through are not meant for us, but to enable us to understand what transpires in other people, so we can help them deal with their conflict, mend hurts and failures they cannot overcome by themselves.

We do not know why we are destined to be in certain places, but God will always plant us in soil to bloom and leave our footprints in the sand for someone else to follow.

THE LAUNCH

All of our children excelled at Calumet High School. Their names also became legends to the faculty, students, and community. They all graduated and enrolled in various universities due to their academic status and athletic abilities. Calumet High School used our family as a role model so much that Theodore Coopwood, III, who attended graduate school and obtained employment with U.S. Fish and Wildlife as an Environmental Biologist, was asked to come back and give a motivational speech to the faculty and all high school students. He received a standing ovation for a speech that stirred and motivated both students and faculty.

God takes our meager beginnings to advance his purpose for our lives. It is not the starting point, but how we use what we have in us to grab the truth of who we are, and who we belong to, then reach down and help someone else find their way to the top. So, it is not how or where you begin, but the ending that counts.

CHILDREN, NO LONGER

As I look at our children, I see their many characteristics, traits and deep level of persistence that was developed because of their struggles to survive in an environment that could have pulled them away from their goals and God given destination. Not having many of the ordinary things in life, they took what they had, used it and saw where they wanted to go and went. They made the best of their schooling by being in activities that would make them stand out from other students. So much so, that their names became legends in both sports and academics for several years after they had graduated. Many times, they expressed feelings of hurt and memories of incidents on paper, but they continued to press on. They excelled in their coursework and participated in activities that exposed them to college experiences and attending a predominantly white school prepared them for their future career paths. Their dad instilled many good principles, one of perseverance, never to quit because it gets hard. He told them they needed to always have to hustle to keep what they earned in life. God blessed all of our children to obtain scholarships and opportunities for college without parental assistance.

All of our children are grown and with fantastic jobs – Two Air Traffic Controllers. One Environmental Biologist, One Industrial Engineer, One Doctorate of Diversity, and One Business Management Entrepreneur. All are entrepreneurs of their own businesses, love God and people so much that they can reach down and pull up the most fallen person and assure them that they can make it if they try. Two now retired, two deceased, leaving their torches to be carried by those left behind.

It does not matter how rough the road, it's with God and your determination that makes one successful. As a mother, I have been awarded one of God's greatest gifts of life, my children. If you stay focused through your trials and keep your family together whatever the cost, God will bring about blessings unimaginable.

MEDITATED DEPARTURE

When the nest is finally empty, God shows us what we could not see before, because we were wrapped up in our turmoil and struggles with trying to simply survive each day. We hang on because we want our family to move forward without remorse. What we don't realize is that children are touched by what they hear, see and our attitudes toward them as parents. When we cannot see them because we are struggling to find ourselves, there is a void and hurt that only God can fill and heal. I am grateful that He did this for all of my children. They learned how to take the good, weed the negative out of their minds leaving only the positive words that have enhanced their lives.

After over fifty (50) years of marriage, life began to be more of a challenge with Ted. His financial instability and domineering attitude were becoming too much for me to bear. I began to think to myself that now, there are no children at home to be concerned about, it is time to begin planning my departure. Ted continued to give himself whole heartily to the community and his company. However, due to his heartfelt desire to help so many people who could not pay him in return, his company failed. His heart was truly into serving others, but he could not see that his first responsibility for service was to his family.

COURAGE TO MOVE

I n the Spring of 2000, after several weeks of slowly packing my car, I drove out of the Small Farms knowing that I would never return. I headed for Knoxville, TN and planned to stay with my daughter who was an Air Traffic Controller at the time and had a home there. As soon as I arrived, I received word that my sister was in the hospital and was not expected to live. I returned to Gary knowing that it would nearly be impossible for me not to see Ted at the funeral. Regardless of me seeing him, I did not waver in my decision and left immediately after the service headed back to Tennessee where I stayed for several months.

After several months of living in Tennessee with my daughter, I began  thinking about the three children with my young grandchildren that lived in Virginia. I decided that I wanted to live as much life with them as I could and at the end of 2000, I moved to Virginia and lived with my middle son and his family.

The first three years in Virginia I lived free of worry, anxiety, fear, physical and mental abuse. I was happy, joyful, and enjoyed the life I was living with my family. I had a car, a job, had affiliated myself with a church to grow spiritually and my life was very good. But little did I know that God's providence was at work and He had the ultimate plan for my life.

My oldest daughter and youngest son took on the responsibility to care for their dad after my departure. They took over and maintained his financial affairs, took care of his medical, housekeeping, and personal needs. After a while it became obvious to them that he was slowly deteriorating mentally and becoming more incapable of taking care of himself when no one was with him. As a result of a few potential life-threatening incidents, the children decided that he needed to move out of the house and be someplace else. They asked him where he wanted to go and he only stated, "I want to go where your mother is." This proposed a problem for them because they knew my situation, but they called me with his request and were willing to do whatever I said. After the call, I thought and labored for several days not really knowing what to do, but I wanted to be right. One night God woke me up about 3am to write a song. I wrote this song called, "Everything". God simply said in a still small voice, "It's not about you, but about me." I simply said, "Ok Lord, then you have to fix it."

When God spoke, it was nothing for me to do but obey, even if it was in haphazard circumstances. This meant breaking up my independence by my own hands, surrendering to the Supremacy of God to make or fix whatever was needed. It was His desire and purpose to do whatever I did not see.

YES LORD!

G od is always true to His Word and always on time! When I told the Lord, He would have to fix it, I was staying with my son and had no place of my own. I needed an apartment of my own, but it also needed to be handicap accessible for Ted. I had applied for Section 8 when I first arrived in Virginia because I was told it took about two years to get placed in a home. Little did I know that my approval for an apartment would come the same time Ted was supposed to arrive in Virginia. The decision to have Ted come was made in June 2001. In July, one month later, I was settled in an apartment, fully furnished by my children, food in the cabinets and rent paid with no extra fees. The man who rented me the apartment was truly an angel from God. He waved several requirements for my benefit and was gone within a week after I moved in.

My sons brought Ted within one week of my moving in. He came into a living condition totally modern, equipped, and comfortable to meet all of his needs. He had a spacious bedroom with a handicap accessible bathroom. This was a different environment, and all he had to do was live with gratefulness.

When Ted first arrived, he was very capable of getting around. We went to church every Sunday and visited our children and grandchildren quite often. I tried to give him my best, but he began to slip back into his old attitude of dominance and control with verbal abuse and manipulation to put fear in me. However, I was now working as a manager of a nursing agency, and I would not respond to his tactics, words or show feelings of fear or anxiety, but would just fix him what he needed and proceed to do what I had planned or needed to do. He soon learned that I was no longer the same person or wife he had back in Gary. I had a totally different view about life, had grown to be my own person by knowing who I was in Christ and had no plans to ever be manipulated by fear or words again!

I, as a human being, had to learn that the power of our individual choices is our responsibility. There are two dates in our life God is in total control of; the day we are born and the day we die. Within these two dates is a line of choices. What we choose is our responsibility and destination. We are always moving, believe it or not, towards either salvation or damnation and we have the power to switch direction at any time. But we definitely cannot change our beginning and ending dates.

When we make the choice to be obedient, the enemy works overtime to push us off the edge. I was determined to stand strong amidst the pressure although things started to get really rough. Ted's knees became so bad that it became difficult for him to walk or even stand any length of time. As a military veteran, he was able to have a knee replacement at the Washington VA Hospital. He remained in the hospital for two weeks and was sent to a rehabilitation center to complete his recovery. While he was at the rehab center, a blood clot formed in his leg and he was sent back to the hospital. This happened because he refused to get up and move around due to the pain.

God is always working and setting what we need in motion, using who we least expect and our immediate circumstances to set our future.

Ted's second trip to the hospital caused him to go to a different rehab center in Arlington, VA. This center was setting up, without my knowledge, Medicare services so he could have a nurse, occupational therapy, medicines, and treatments from the VA. He remained in rehab for about three weeks and became able to move around with a walker for short distances. This allowed him to be discharged to come home. I was advised that all the services and assistance Ted needed was already arranged and would be provided. When he came home, he had a nurse assistant for 8-hours each day and therapy twice a week. The therapy only lasted 2-weeks because Ted would not cooperate when the therapist tried to get him to exercise or even walk a short distance. He would never try to walk on his own but always insisted on using the walker. After a while, he became totally dependent on people helping him at all times. This became problematic for me because many times he would fall, and I would have to call either one of my sons or the paramedic to pick him up off the floor. Nevertheless, I continued to take him to church, to our children's house and various activities that I thought he would like. The elevator in our apartment building made transporting very easy. I would take him down in his wheelchair, and then he would use the walker to get in the car. When reaching the destination, other people would assist him out of the car and help him stand to use his walker or get in his wheelchair. This was our life routine for several years until his dementia began to worsen.

As Ted's dementia worsened, his disposition became challenging at times when trying to assist him with personal care. He would refuse to cooperate, be stubborn or get defensive and try to physically grab hold of the caregiver. This resulted in several changes in nursing assistants over the years. In addition to the emotional changes caused by dementia, there were physical changes as well. Ted became 100% incontinent and had a permanent catheter inserted in his abdomen. This procedure required his nursing hours to be increased to twelve a day and a monthly visit to the doctor so the catheter could be changed. This became a hardship on me because Ted was paranoid about the catheter because he did not really understand why it was there. He would get defensive when the nurse tried to care for it, so I found myself doing most of his personal hygiene care to avoid any physical incidents.

God gave me more patience than I ever knew I had. The most profound thing I realized was that I could listen to Ted belittle me and say all kinds of ugly things, but I never felt like I did not want to help him. The eviler he became, the more I did for him. He had everything he needed;

with nothing missing. God blessed me so that I could continue to show love in spite of his attitude. I had to remember that his heart was good, even if he spoke from his mind, which was diseased.

When Ted was at peace, he would always talk about God and what he wanted for his children. He could not imagine them as adults with families, but he still felt he had to work for them. When I would remind him that they were grown and he did not need to think about work, it would trigger such an explosion, that I learned to just let him talk without saying anything.

THE START TO THE END

After suffering for over 11 years with a bad knee, I had a knee replacement. This created a problem because someone needed to be with Ted at night after the nurse assistant went home. The nurse stayed from 8am to 8pm and I would take over all of his care until the next morning. My daughter had a friend who was willing to come and stay with Ted until I was able to come back to the apartment. She came several days before the time to get acquainted with him so he would be comfortable with her in the home. After my knee surgery, I was in rehab for a week and then stayed at my son's house for an additional two weeks. My daughter's friend had several nights of unrest while staying at the apartment with Ted because he kept coming into her bedroom looking for me.

One night, during my last week at my son's house, Ted became so paranoid and afraid that he locked himself in his room. He pushed his scooter to the door and fell over it hard to the floor. My daughter's friend heard the loud noise but could not get in the room. When the nurse assistant arrived and could not get a response from Ted or get in the room, she called the Paramedics. The Paramedics called the fire department so they could use a ladder to get in the window because our apartment was on the second floor. Once the door was opened, the Paramedics picked Ted up and set him on the bed, stating he should go to the hospital. The nurse assistant stated that him falling was not unusual, so the Paramedics left him sitting on the bed. After several hours with Ted refusing to stand or move and complaining that his leg was hurting, the friend called my daughter, who then came and picked me up and we went to the apartment. He immediately said to me, "I can't stand up." By his expression, I knew he was really hurting. I called his doctor and was told to send him to the hospital. Ted was admitted with a fracture in his right leg. After a week in the hospital, the doctor and hospital administration decided to send him to Manassas Rehab. and Nursing Facility. This Rehab was very patient with him, even when he would act threatening or refuse to cooperate in any way. This became Ted's new permanent home.

Ted refused to rehabilitate even using a walker. He was content in being confined to the wheelchair and classified as a Nursing Home resident. He quickly became liked by the staff and many of the visitors. When he was not agitated, he would talk and shake hands with everyone he met. The staff became familiar with his mood swings and how to handle his emotions. There were some nurses he would respond to and they could get him to calm down easier than others. They managed him by keeping the nurses he was familiar with at or near his station area.

While Ted was in the nursing home, he never missed anything that the family planned. The children would get him for holidays and special events. They would prepare a ramp for his wheelchair when bringing him to their homes and even hire a nurse to take care of his hygiene needs so I would not have to do it. My oldest son Teddy, was only ten minutes from the facility and he would visit almost every day, kept him shaved and cut his hair. Ted was never without visitors between my children, grandchildren, or me. The men from the church would sometimes come and pick him up. They would also pay for transportation to escort him to church and back to the facility. This was done on several occasions and the last time was for his ninetieth birthday to attend a dinner and party.

In the beginning of 2017, Ted's activity started to slow down, and he began to stay in bed most of the time. Many people would just come into his room just to speak to him. His temperament changed and was quiet, and he became the star of the facility. All of the staff and visitors would talk about him having a kind heart, talking mostly about God and his family. On Saturday July 15, 2017 right after lunch, he was sitting in the hallway talking to his favorite nurse and stated he was tired. When she turned her head to get some medication, then turned back around, he was slumped down in his wheelchair. She called for help and they put him in the bed but, eternity was his time. He had now passed from death to life.

MIRRORED HEARTS

The night of February 4, 2018, seven months after Ted's death, I was lying in bed unable to sleep listening to praise and worship music. God began to move within my spirit, and I began to think about Ted. I heard the Spirit of God say to me, "He was like a David to me. He had warred all his life, but he had a heart for God. "Yes, he became a man of war as a result of his early fight in life, but he had the one quality I desired most. This had been his focal point even through all of his difficulties in life. He lived what he believed; to be strong and war in his defense, but his heart was always upon me". At that moment, my spirit became so overwhelmed that tears began to flow, with my simple statement, "Yes Lord, thank you". It was such a revelation that I searched the Bible for the comparison of these two men. One living many centuries ago, one just recently entered into eternity. Looking at both of their lives, the pattern unfolded. Rejection in childhood, determined to fight and win at all costs, loved God's word, and never doubted it regardless of the difficulty that was faced. Standing on the word was their daily bread that sustained them in fulfillment of both life and death. Everyone knew that God was the source that they depended upon. Theodore's last words were about the blessings of God upon himself and his family.

By God showing me the amazing resemblance between David and Ted, it helped me really see and understand the things that mattered most. It is not our struggles, hurts, or failures but the commitment of our heart that matters. Do we have a heart for God? This is what He wants from all of us; our heart no matter what circumstances we find ourselves in. If our hearts are not in tune with God so He can heal and deliver us, then we have missed the purpose of living.

Only God knows what lives in our hearts; that part that no man sees.

The mind is so imaginary that we take what we hear and build our lives on things we assume.

Miracles Manifested

The following occurrences are true because I either experienced them personally or they were told to me by someone who I believe would not lie about how God blessed their life.

REASSURANCE OF SALVATION

It has now been several weeks since the passing of my brother Walter. My mother was still in a state of mourning and asking, "Lord, did he make it into your kingdom?".

One night or day, I really do not know because I have no date or time of the occurrence. Like the Apostle Paul stated, "Whether in the body or out of the body I cannot tell." I do know for a positive fact; I was sitting in the kitchen on a bar stool at the counter when my brother appeared. I looked directly at him, talked, and questioned him about his dying. I told him about being buried. He stated, "I know you buried me, but I am not dead." I proceeded to tell him that he did not have any clothes because my mother had his suits and pants remade for me. He replied, "Where I am, I don't need clothes. The Lord saved me just in time." Before I could speak another word, he vanished. I cannot or will not try to explain a form or figure because it was something indescribable, but it was as real as I am writing this. There was never a question or doubt in my mind about God or eternity after death afterwards.

After this encounter, I told my mother about Walter's visit. She immediately stopped worrying and began to smile. I knew the message was for her as well as me. But I was the instrument in which it came. This happened in 1949 when I was eighteen and to this day, I have not seen Walter again.

My mother, who is now with the Lord, told me of this encounter she had years after Walter had died and I was much older. She was ill and confined to bed and could feel the breath of hot air on her cheek and a small voice whispered, " I am as close to you as the air you breathe'". She told me that she immediately recognized the voice and called my brother's name.

Only God brings the unveiling at his appointed time. He lets us know that He and His Kingdom are real. There is truly a hereafter, and how we live on planet earth does matter.

DIVINE PROTECTION

In 1956, a car of teenagers heading Northbound on Route 20 lost control of their vehicle, crossed the median and hit my mother's cab that was traveling Southbound on Route 20. There were two other passengers in the back seat of the cab. The head-on collision caused my mother to have the most trauma because she was pinned under the steering wheel. She incurred broken ribs, both legs broken with her knees crushed, and many lacerations. My stepdad, who was sitting on the passenger's side, only had a dislocated hip. One of the passengers in the back had face and eye injuries. Unfortunately, two of the teenagers in the other car died. Ironically, my mother was only on Route 20 because of a construction detour.

My stepfather, after a week in the hospital and getting ready to be discharged for home, was finally able to see my mother in her room. He told her that he was going home the next day and not to worry but, just get well and he would take care of everything.

My stepfather went back to his room, went to bed and died that night. A blood clot had formed and traveled to his heart as a result of him getting up to go and see my mother. My sister and I did not know how to break this news to our mom who was still lying on her back with her leg up in traction. My sister made a radical statement, "Let's not tell her, we will just bury him because we don't want to make her worse." I stated," We cannot do this, she will never forgive us, she has a right to know!"

When we went to the hospital very early and entered Mom's room, she immediately said, " What is wrong, why are you here?" We could sense that she felt something, so we told her about Clisby passing that night after coming to see her. She took it calmly, saying, "Oh, Lord!". She told us what to do and where to find everything we needed. We followed her instructions and took care of all the arrangements with her guidance. She was pleased even though she could not attend the funeral. She trusted God and knew that everything would be alright.

After several weeks, Mom was able to come home but was told because her kneecaps were so badly damaged she would never walk again. My mother believed that God would restore her, and she would make a full recovery. God blessed and totally healed her knees, and she was able to walk without using a walker or cane. She closed her store and started a new life. She lived a full life working in church, becoming responsible for many community activities, coordinating weddings and traveling to many places abroad and in the States. She lived until the age of eighty-six (86) with no regrets.

My mother was a firm believer, with unshakeable faith, knowing all things work together for good in God's timing. She believed that God was always controlling what we can't see.

CARRIED HOME

After working a book table sale in Indianapolis, Indiana and returning home with a trunk loaded with books, I heard a loud noise like the tire had blown out. I continued to drive but slowed down because I thought I had a flat tire, but I continued to drive. About a half a mile from Lafayette, I pulled over at a truck stop and noticed that the trimming on the tire on the passenger side was gone. The tire was still up, so I continued to drive home since I only had 20 minutes left before reaching the house. After getting home, I told my husband about the tire and he went outside to look at it and asked me how I was able to drive on the tire. When I looked at the tire, the front tire was flat, but the back tire was completely shredded.

We find daily that God works all things for our good even when we cannot see Him in them.

THEODORE AND EMILY'S CHILDREN

Janet

S trong, courageous and has pressed through many obstacles throughout her life. She was a young mother but was always determined to succeed regardless of her circumstances. She established a deep relationship with God early in her life and He has been the rock that sustained her through many storms in her life. Janet has always had the ability to speak into the lives of others not only giving advice but helping them think and seek the best solutions for their situations. She is an advocate and supporting confidant for her family and makes herself available whenever needed. She excelled early in her career regardless of the hardships she faced as a result of being raised in a "can do" home environment and believing that with God all things were possible. She always served God in ministry wherever she lived and although never ordained as a minister, she served as a youth leader, Sunday school superintendent, praise and worship leader, Ministry of Helps and Administration, Prison Ministry and several other positions where needed.

Janet completed graduate school and went on to be selected Manager of two FAA Flight Service Facilities before retiring as a federal employee after 27 years of service. She continues to serve others today by owning her own business Leadership with Purpose and Passion by assisting others in enhancing their leadership and managerial skills.

Pamela

Pamela is dedicated to believing in her God. She is diligent, dedicated to success despite the difficulties encountered, she persevered. The pressures of life have made her resilient and fierce in the pursuit of her God and her life goals. She embodies the motto enshrined by her Father to "Never say can't!". Her devotion to her ABBA Father and his unconditional love kept her striving to reach her potential, study hard and be her own person regardless of doubt and criticism. She retired from the FAA as an Air Traffic Manager and then accomplished two MBA's, first in Event Management and then in Theology. She has served God internationally as a Missionary, speaking and disciplining in over twenty-five countries. She has been CEO of her own company, The Planned Event, for over twenty years, and now devotes her life to Chaplaincy and pursuing her life-long desire to show the love of God to those who are hurt and marginalized in life.

Theodore III

Quiet, hates confusion and has many wounds and scars from childhood and adult life. God has been and continues to be his greatest strength, refuge and comfort in overcoming. He has pressed through many challenges, learning how to cope and think to determine his destiny.

He loves God, wife Teresa, and his family, and he is now a great motivational speaker for church, community, his job as well as schools. He was hired as a Biologist for EPA after graduating from college, obtained a master's degree in Biology and has traveled throughout the US. He is a great athlete, stressing bodybuilding, running and working out daily himself.

Gregory (Deceased)

Gregory was a mighty warrior for God! He was known for being a hard worker with the ability to accomplish anything he set his mind to do. He was a true servant of humanity in his lifetime. The passion he had for helping others was unmatched by most. Greg, "Coop" or "G" as some would call him, was family oriented and raised his children to love and trust God in all things. He demonstrated his faith in his home and to others by his actions.

Greg was always available when he was needed regardless of the distance or the request. His smile was contagious, and it showed even when he disagreed. Greg was gifted with knowing how to analyze things by just looking at them. There was nothing he could not build or repair. He had a schooling in industrial engineering and worked as a contractor in foreign governments and many major companies. His gift went well beyond what he learned in school; it was from God. He lived to own his own business, Industrial Consultant of Maintenance Management (ICMM, Inc.), which proved to be a blessing to the hundreds that were served. Lastly, he was gifted with superhuman strength that he used to glorify God by serving others.

Kenny

This was the child that seemed to have the least amount of conflict while growing into adulthood. He was always shielded by his older brothers, and he was always held in high regard by people at his schools. He was soft-spoken about most of life's sensitive matters and determined not to struggle as he saw his father and other men do to survive. He always thought about what choices he could make to prevent struggle. As he worked alongside his father, he learned how things and the world worked. He learned many lessons from the hard work he endured and applied those lessons well. Most significantly, he learned early to study his pathway to success, stick to his beliefs, and apply what he learned. He remains today very observant and conscientious about his studies and his surroundings. He mentors young boys and inspires them to be excellent at being their best. He earned a doctorate in educational administration, leadership, and foundations, a master's in public administration, and a bachelor's degree with an emphasis in finance, marketing, and management without paying for either degree. He has worked in several universities and served as a vice president in three states. He now owns a nationally recognized consulting firm where he works with people, colleges, and universities across the country. He is still soft-spoken but roars with care and courage, humor, and wisdom.

Deborah

My last child, and third daughter Deborah, was a courageous woman determined to succeed. A visionary from her youth, she refused to be dissuaded by negativity or deterred by dissenting opinions. Her life, plagued by illness and physical limitations, produced hardships from an early age. Even as a young adult, she continued to struggle, but refused to be hampered by these limitations. Although she juggled her diverse talents against her feelings of self-worth, she persevered in her love of all things theatrical. She adored her brother Kenneth with whom she shared the last years of home life. But although they were close in age, they eventually separated because their choice in friends, academics, and social circles was vastly different. Driven by feelings of perceived favoritism toward his accomplishments, acrimony caused Deborah to feel unloved, abandoned, and impoverished for affection. After leaving home immediately after graduation, she fully blossomed into the beautiful young lady she was destined to be. Her gifts of theatrical performance, her commanding vocals, and her zeal for life took her from the moors of Gary, Indiana, to the shimmering coast of California. The one love of her life produced a daughter, Cecile. Before her early death, her world celebrated her gifts as a songstress, radio producer, and creative director. Her memoir in tribute is a heartfelt CD rendition of her singing, "Wind Beneath My Wings."

A Letter to Mothers

The most important responsibility God gave to mankind is procreation. God created and chose women to birth, nurture and raise children. Women are the bedrock of the world because what we teach and instill in our children ultimately determines the condition of the world in which we all live. The divine connection that starts in the womb creates a direct channel for sharing love, attitudes, thoughts and emotions between a child and a mother. It is similar to our hearts being transformed by the love of God and His Spirit living within us.

The journey of motherhood is so important, that I have chosen to tell my story of what I have learned in my years of being a parent, grandparent and now a great-grandparent. If we as mothers miss the purpose of the seed, our children, and fail to nourish them so they properly grow and develop in the image of God, then they will ultimately grow into adulthood not knowing their divine purpose for which they were born. Children who are not properly nurtured, find it difficult if not impossible to determine their purpose in life, understand what is desired of them and many times fall prey to the whims of the society in which they live. We do not always see that we already have enough for our children just by being who we are to them, their parents. What they need from us most of all is relationships.

Each child is different and requires specific personal attention. It is not the material things we can give them but the love, cuddling and listening moments that makes them feel special. Each child has a different nature, their own ideas, and levels of understanding. A mother must learn how to study and observe each child, discover their strengths and challenges, and know how to help each one move forward. The comments of praise and approval of their accomplishments regardless how small or insignificant you might think of it, gives a child confidence in themselves. We must realize that every child has a purpose, and it is our responsibility to instill hard work, encourage them to study and be prepared, and never accept the word "can't" but teaching that nothing is impossible with God.

As flawed human beings with a lack of understanding of the human heart, we will never get it all right as a mother or even as parents. Motherhood is an endless journey, and every woman who has children will have a story! I struggled with many high and low points and had to trust God in making hard decisions. My children were wounded by their father but also by me as their mother because I did not see them as individuals. They carried the scars into adulthood that could only be healed by God and my apologies. If a child has been wounded or rejected by anything a mother has said or done to them, they will carry the hurt into adulthood which will impact how they love and mature. If this is part of your story, apologize so the healing can begin.

When we do our best in nurturing and raising our children using the directions that God provided, He will continue to build on that foundation and finish the work in their lives.

Along our journey in life,
we develop our story,
in the process of time on this earth,
having faith in the supernatural
as we walk in the natural,
allowing our faith to dominate
early in our walk,
to learn how to discern the
real from the unreal,
and not being deceived by
the enemy of our spirit.

Emily Janet Robinson Coopwood